For over 500 years there has been a pala ~~~~ ~~~. 1 11st came the Tudor palace, built by Edward Seymour, Duke of Somerset and virtual ruler, as Lord Protector of England, in the minority of his nephew, Edward VI, son of Henry VIII. Then, for nearly 200 years, the palace saw important political and cultural events through the reigns of five queens: two Tudor Queens, Mary and Elizabeth; and three Stuart Queens, Anne of Denmark, Henrietta Maria and Catharine of Braganza.

By the 18th century the palace was in ruins, used as a shabby lodging house for servants of the crown. George III exchanged it with his government for Buckingham Palace and the government decided to rebuild it as a headquarters for offices of state, including the Navy Board. George III also granted room for three learned societies, the Royal Academy of Arts, the Royal Society and the Society of Antiquaries.

This is the present building. It is the most outstanding 18th-century public building in London.

By the early part of the 20th century, Somerset House had been entirely taken over by the Civil Service and was almost unknown to the public. But, over the past twelve years a substantial part of Somerset House has been opened up for all to enjoy. The Courtauld Institute of Art is one of the world's leading art collections. There are dancing fountains in the Edmond J. Safra Fountain Court which is used as an an open-air cinema and for outdoor gigs in the summer and for skating in the winter. There are challenging contemporary exhibitions in the Embankment Galleries all year round. Small cultural and artistic enterprises are now moving into the former Civil Service offices, enriching the third age of Somerset House, which is enjoying a renaissance as a contemporary cultural palace; an 18th-century jewel in the crown of London, capital city of culture in the 21st century.

'I write some lines in the solitude of Somerset House not fifty yards from the Thames on one side and the Strand on the other, but quiet as the sands of Arabia' *George Crabbe (1754–1832) Diary, August 1817*

I

THE ROYAL PALACE

Somerset House was built as a grand riverside palace by ambitious Edward Seymour, 1st Duke of Somerset, but his execution for treason in 1552 saw his unfinished palace appropriated by the crown.

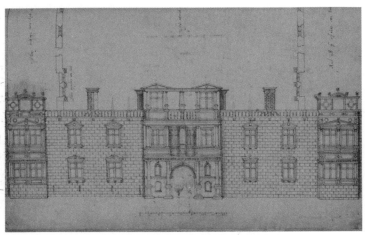

Elevation of Strand front,
by John Thorpe, *circa* 1603
© Sir John Soane's Museum

THE LORD PROTECTOR, DUKE OF SOMERSET

Edward Seymour, born in about 1506, was a member of the new nobility created by King Henry VIII to counter-balance the influence of the church, one of those *nouveaux riches* who benefited financially by the proceeds of the dissolution of the monasteries.

By 1530, having fought in successful battles in France for which he was knighted, Seymour became an esquire of the King's body and enjoyed a close friendship with Henry. His sister, Lady Jane Seymour was also at court, first as Maid of Honour to Catherine of Aragon and then to

Anne Boleyn. When the King started to become interested in Jane, her ambitious brother paved the way. Anne Boleyn was beheaded in May 1536; two weeks later Henry married Jane. In October 1537, after the birth of their son Edward, Seymour was created Earl of Hertford. The death of his sister, ten days after she had given birth to the future King, was a blow to her brother. He was described at the time as a man 'young and wise but of small power'. However, he remained friends with the King and, three years later, having successfully defended and fortified Calais and Guines, he was given Chester Place, outside Temple Bar, London, and the site of the future Somerset House,

formerly the property of the church in the name of the Bishop of Chester.

Henry's death in January 1547 left Hertford, uncle to the new young King Edward VI, pre-eminent. He at once took possession of the royal will by hurrying to Hatfield to assume control of the young king. Hertford assumed 'the name and title of Protector of all the realms and domains of the King's Majesty and governor of his most royal person'. He was created Duke of Somerset by Edward VI and became virtual ruler during his nephew's minority.

To accommodate his new position, the Duke decided to build a new palace on the Strand – which was becoming a strand of palaces, those of York, Durham, Exeter, Savoy and Arundel. To make room for his new palace, the Protector demolished the religious buildings on and around the site, not only to clear the land but to provide the brick and stone he needed for his new palace. That fiery preacher, John Knox, observed at the time that he preferred 'watching the masons to listening to sermons'.

It is not known who designed the Lord Protector's new palace. John Thorpe has been put forward and certainly he drew sketches of the palace when virtually complete. The author of a *Critical View of Buildings* (1734) wrote 'I am extremely pleased with the front of the first court of Somerset House as it affords us a view of the first dawning of taste in England' It was the first building in England to acknowledge the influence of the Renaissance.

QUEEN ELIZABETH I

After Somerset's impeachment and death in 1552 his new, as yet unfinished, palace was appropriated by the Crown and given to Princess Elizabeth, who would have preferred Durham House. When she became Queen in 1558, she favoured the palaces at Whitehall or St James's but used the palace for meetings of her council and to lodge a series of foreign diplomats sent to negotiate for her hand in marriage. These included Philibert of Savoy, the Duke of Holstein on behalf of Frederick II of Denmark and the Marshal of France on behalf of the Duc d'Alençon. In 1575, she gave the palace into the keeping of her cousin, Lord Hunsdon, and after he died, to his widow for a fee of 12d. a day and the garden for a fee of 6d. a day. The palace went to sleep.

QUEEN ANNE OF DENMARK

In 1603, James VI of Scotland succeeded Elizabeth as James I of England and brought his cultivated Queen, Anne of Denmark, to London. Under her patronage Denmark House, as it was now called, became the cultural and social centre of English life. Anne promoted the development of the English masque, employing the poet Ben Jonson to write the masques and Inigo Jones to design their sets and costumes. She often appeared in these extravagant entertainments herself, dancing in Ben Jonson's *Masque of Christmas*,

Portrait of Queen Elizabeth I, when a princess, *circa* 1547–58
Anglo-Italian School, 16th century
© Philip Mould Ltd, London /
The Bridgeman Art Library

for instance. From 1609, Anne also embarked on a major reconstruction of the palace, Inigo Jones being responsible for rebuilding and adding to existing buildings and rendering the riverfront in stone. This work continued until her death in 1619.

left: Portrait of Edward Seymour, 1st Duke of Somerset, 9 January 1541
Reproduced by permission of the Marquess of Bath, Longleat House, Warminster, Wiltshire
© Marquess of Bath

right: Anne of Denmark, *circa* 1605–10
attributed to Marcus Gheeraerts
© Woburn Abbey, Bedfordshire / Bridgeman Art Library

The Somerset House Conference, 1604, by unknown artist © National Portrait Gallery, London

THE EARLIEST INTERIOR OF SOMERSET HOUSE

This is the only known image of the interior of the royal palace of Somerset House, over sixty years after the Duke of Somerset had originally commissioned it. It is probably true that this interior had scarcely changed during the intervening reign of Elizabeth I, as the palace had hardly been used by her Court and was thus not grandly furnished nor altered. Because the Somerset House Conference was so important, and James I parsimonious, he enriched the shabby Council Chamber with borrowed tapestries from the royal collection in Whitehall and covered the conference table with a carpet also from Whitehall. The tapestries were 'the most gorgeous hangings that belong to the Crown' and formed part of the huge collection of Henry VIII. It is difficult to see their subjects in this painting, but almost certainly they were part of the sale

I   THE ROYAL PALACE

THE SOMERSET HOUSE CONFERENCE

The peace treaty, ending almost 20 years of war between England, Spain and the Spanish Netherlands, known as The Treaty of London, was signed at Somerset House in 1604. For reasons of prestige, the Spanish Ambassador insisted that the meeting of the visitors, headed by Juan de Velasco, Duke of Frias and Constable of Castile, take place at Somerset House, which had been mothballed during the last years of the reign of Elizabeth I's reign. Suitable apartments were furnished by the King with his best possessions and other furnishings borrowed from neighbouring palaces. Anxious to impress the Commissioners with as many liveried servants as possible, but wanting no more expense than the £300 a day that the visit was going to cost him, King James hastily summoned Shakespeare and his company of actors, who had previously been appointed King's Company of Players and provided with a livery on the occasion of the Coronation procession.

QUEEN HENRIETTA MARIA

Charles I came to the throne in 1625, and later that year was married by proxy to Henrietta Maria of France – a devout Roman Catholic. The next year, the new queen became entitled to the use of Denmark House and Inigo Jones continued to make alterations and improvements to the palace. He designed new decorative fixtures to the Queen's closet, a new river-gate and stairs and a new Cabinet Room. But by far the most important work that took place was the Queen's Chapel, described as 'a lavish setting for the mass'. Such encouragement by the King to allow his Queen to build a catholic chapel did much to encourage the growing clashes between King and Parliament, which ended with the Civil War and the establishment of the Commonwealth.

During the Civil War, Denmark House was used as a headquarters for General Fairfax, commander of the Parliamentary army.

King Charles I and his family
School of Sir Anthony van Dyck
© Royal Hospital Chelsea, London

of the King's Goods 45 years later. Almost a century old by 1604, the carpet on the table is of the 'small-Holbein' pattern; there are mentions of it in Henry VIII's inventories. The chairs are covered in silks and velvets and were borrowed from the Duke of Dorset, who owned the neighbouring Arundel House.

Archduke Leopold Wilhelm in his Picture Gallery, *circa* 1647, by David Teniers the Younger © Prado, Madrid

THE SALE OF THE KING'S GOODS

After the beheading of Charles I at Whitehall in 1649, Cromwell decided to sell off the Royal Collection, partly to pay the army and the navy but also to symbolise the stripping of temporal power from the institution of royalty.

A great part of this extraordinary collection – amassed in the main by Charles I, but some of which he had inherited from his royal forebears – was now taken from the royal palaces, especially Whitehall, carefully inventoried and displayed at Denmark House. Everything was stripped down and shipped, down to the smallest cooking utensils. It was the greatest ever sale of a private collection.

There were 1,760 pictures alone, with works by Leonardo da Vinci, Giorgione, Raphael and Michelangelo; there were numerous masterpieces by Correggio, Titian, Tintoretto, Holbein and Van Dyck, together with magnificent tapestries, furniture, even the robes of Henry VIII, and unused bolts of cloth and trimmings, from the splendour and magnificence of six reigns.

The crowned heads of Europe and rich Dutch merchants sent anonymous agents to buy these treasures, but the whole sale was badly mismanaged by the corrupt and self-interested former royal servants put in its charge. Corruption, bribery and chicanery over the four years of its dispersement led to some

Oliver Cromwell Lying in State, *circa* 1658, English School © Private Collection / The Bridgeman Art Library

astonishingly low prices for some of the great masterpieces of the Italian High Renaissance, favoured by Charles I. These, such as Leonardo da Vinci's *St John the Baptist*, which went to the French royal family, were dispersed to the courts of Europe; few were recovered after the Restoration.

THE RESTORATION

Cromwell died in 1658, and at Somerset House his effigy lay in state for many weeks after his death. The diarist and royalist John Evelyn recalled, 'It was the joyfullest funeral I ever saw; for there were none that cried but dogs....'

After Charles II's eventual restoration in 1660, his mother, Queen Henrietta Maria, returned to Somerset House and it was during her last years here that a riverfront gallery was built with five open arches and sculptured keystones. It provided inspiration for Sir William Chambers when he designed the Strand frontage of the new Somerset House in the late 1770s.

In 1665, Henrietta Maria returned to France to escape the Plague, as the diarist Samuel Pepys recalled in his entry for 29th June: 'Home, calling at Somerset House where all were packing up, too; the Queen Mother setting out for France this day'. She never returned to her palace, dying in France four years later.

QUEEN CATHERINE OF BRAGANZA

Charles II's Portuguese queen was quiet, dowdy, devoutly Roman Catholic and became the last royal resident of Somerset House. While her husband led a profligate Court at St James's with his reigning mistresses, Queen Catherine led a quieter and simpler life at Somerset House; the splendours of Henrietta Maria's reign were only a memory. The lavishly decorated rooms now contained sombre religious pictures and the crowd of courtiers and servants had dwindled to a small entourage who played quiet games of cards with their queen. After Charles

died in 1685, the Dowager Queen lived quietly in the reign of William and Mary, but was the focus point for Roman Catholic proselytising in her adopted country. In 1693, she was asked to become the Regent of Portugal and finally went home.

From then on, Somerset House sank into obscurity. No longer a royal palace, and a large royal household filled with grand visitors and courtiers, it slumbered quietly, providing Grace and Favour apartments to indigent relatives and friends in the gift of the monarch, such as the 2nd Earl of Clarendon who lived in apartments in the gatehouse. Somerset House dreamed of other, more glorious days.

St John the Baptist, 1513–16, by Leonardo da Vinci was part of the Royal Collection © Louvre, Paris

Catherine of Braganza, *circa* 1660–1661, by or after Dirk Stoop © National Portrait Gallery, London

II
MASQUES, MASQUERADES, REVELS AND ROUTS

In the 16th century, masques became complicated allegories, often very flattering to their patrons. The artistically-inclined Anne of Denmark raised them to a very sophisticated art form, dancing in them herself.

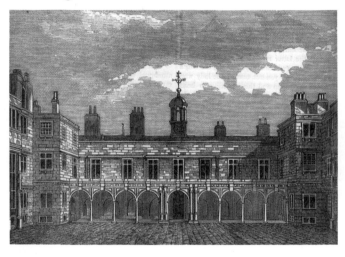

above: Inigo Jones, 1757–58
by William Hogarth
© National Maritime Museum, London

left: The Court of Old Somerset House
from the north, 17th century
© Antiquarian Images

MASQUES

The masques performed at Denmark House, as Somerset House became known in the time of Anne of Denmark, were extremely elaborate – and very expensive, combining music, verse and décor, often with elaborate transformation scenes, specially-designed costumes and dance.

Much of the music was composed by Ferrabosco, the verse was written by Ben Jonson and other poets, while the scenes and costumes were designed by Inigo Jones, who first became prominent through his work on these masques. This collaboration began in 1605, when Jonson's first attempt, *The Masque of Blacknesse*, was performed. It consisted of a backcloth, stage lighting and mobile scenery, which included the moving waves of a simulated ocean in which rolled an enormous shell; sea

opposite page:
Inigo Jones' masque drawings

above: A Fiery Spirit from *The Lord's Masque*; A Daughter of Niger from *The Masque of Blacknesse*; A Star from *The Lord's Masque*

below: Back Shutter for a Landscape

© Devonshire Collection, Chatsworth. Reproduced by permission of Chatsworth Settlement Trustees

8

Interior view of Somerset House showing figures dressed for a masquerade, 1805, after William Hogarth
© Guildhall Library, City of London / The Bridgeman Art Library

Princess Augusta, by Jean-Baptiste
van Loo (1684–1745) © The Trustees
of the Goodwood Collection /
The Bridgeman Art Library

George II, by George Knapton (1698–1778) /
Bank of England, London, UK
© Heini Schneebeli / The Bridgeman Art Library

monsters and water nymphs carried
smaller shells illuminated by lights.
Overhead was a night sky set with
glittering stars and a moon goddess
spoke her part from a throne in
the heavens.

Even as late as 1640, when Anne
had been dead for over twenty years,
the masques continued. When her
son Charles I's quarrel with Parliament
was reaching its height, Inigo Jones
stage-managed his last production.
This was the masque *Salmacida
Spolia*, in which the King himself,
dressed in silver and satin and the
Queen, impersonating an Amazon,
descended from heaven to rout the
evil spirits of rebellion.

MASQUERADES

In 1712 the duc d'Aumont, the French Ambassador who lived in one of the Grace and Favour apartments in the fast-crumbling palace, gave the first of a series of grand masquerades for some 600 guests at the palace. A masquerade was, in effect, the forerunner of today's masked ball, and in the 18th century these could become very riotous indeed, as Addison reported in the 21 May 1716 issue of the *Freeholder*: '... during his progress through the Strand... seeing a great many in rich morning gowns, he was amazed to find that persons of quality were up so early... a hackney coach chancing to pass by him, four Batts popped out their heads all at once which very much frightened both him and his horse'.

In 1749, the palace saw the Jubilee subscription masquerade attended by King George II and Augusta, Princess of Wales. One of the sensations of this gathering was the appearance 'in an almost primitive state' of Elizabeth Chudleigh, a beautiful Maid of Honour, later Duchess of Kingston. In a letter to Sir Horace Mann, Horace Walpole said, 'Miss Chudleigh was Iphigienia, but so naked you would have taken her for Andromeda'.

In 1763 the Venetian Ambassador made a grand entry into London and was entertained at Somerset House with a masque of regal magnificence; this was perhaps the last occasion on which the palace recaptured its vanished glory and became the home of pageantry.

ROUTS

Routs were a great feature of 18th-century social life. Beginning in the mid-evening and continuing into the early hours, they were very sociable events offering gambling, dancing and gossip. Guests first ate their dinners at home, and were then offered pudding and sweets with wine and champagne at the rout.

In 1985, for just one night, the glorious parties from Somerset House's past were revived for a Georgian Rout in aid of The Georgian Society. Beautifully-costumed guests arrived in carriages-and-four and sedan chairs to gamble and dance in the rooms in the Gatehouse formerly occupied by the Royal Academy and turned, for the evening, into a series of gaming rooms and rooms for *conversazione.*

Portrait of Louis Marie Augustin d'Aumont (1709–1782). Reproduced by kind permission of the Ville de Boulogne-sur-Mer

Elizabeth Chudleigh, Duchess of Kingston as she appeared at the Jubilee subscription masquerade in Somerset House, engraved by Francis Chesham, after Thomas Gainsborough © Private Collection / The Bridgeman Art Library

Old Somerset House from the River Thames, circa 1746–50, by Canaletto © Private Collection / The Bridgeman Art Library

III
THE ARCHITECTURE OF A PALACE

By the 1770s, having been mothballed for over a century, Somerset House was in ruins. A visitor at the time wrote that it was 'a correct picture of those dilapidated castles, the haunts of spectres and residence of magicians and murderers'.

above: Sir William Chambers by Sir Joshua Reynolds, 1780 © Royal Academy of Arts

NATIONAL SPLENDOUR

In May 1774, the Board of Works reported that large parts of the palace were about to collapse. A few days later, King George III agreed with his government to exchange it for Buckingham House. The government immediately decided on its total demolition and commissioned a new building to house a number of government offices that were scattered around the palace of Whitehall and its environs, together with the principal learned societies insisted on by the King.

To house several important government departments in a purpose-built building was an extremely modern concept; hitherto each had had its own building. At first, the notion was simply to erect a functional building, but Parliament debated this, and suggested that 'so vast and expensive a design should be at once an object of national splendour as well as convenience.'

Curiously, the commission did not initially go to Sir William Chambers, architect and Comptroller of the Office of Works, who had declared an interest in the project, but to one of his subordinates, William Robinson, the Secretary of the Board of Works and Clerk of Somerset House. While Parliament was debating the exact terms of the commission, Robinson died and Chambers was given the task. The buildings were to be 'erected in a plain manner rather with a view to convenience than ornament...' the work was to be executed with the 'strictest attention to the business of the Public offices; but likewise with an eye to the Ornament of the Metropolis and as a monument of the taste and elegance of His Majesty's reign'.

View of Somerset House on the Thames River, 1802–1806, by William Daniell
© Historical Picture Archive / CORBIS

THE REQUIREMENTS OF THE BUILDING

Chambers' design had to accommodate the three principal learned societies, the Royal Academy of Arts, the Royal Society and the Society of Antiquaries, the housing of which had been part of King George III's deal with the government. He also had to provide space for various other government offices, and in particular the Navy Board, whose new headquarters at Somerset House would thus be conveniently on the river, therefore making the dockyards and warehouses at Greenwich and Deptford easily accessible. The building had also to reflect the rising importance of the Navy at a time when Britain was almost constantly at war.

OFFICES AND LIVING QUARTERS

The new building also had to contain living accommodation for the heads of the various departments housed there, and this meant space for their cooks, housekeepers and secretaries as well as storage space.

Chambers resolved these needs by treating the offices and living accommodation as a series of town houses arranged around a great central courtyard. Each department was allocated a vertical slice of six storeys – cellar, basement, ground floor, first floor, attic and garret. There were two storeys in the basement and one in the roof so that above ground the buildings appeared no more than three storeys high. In addition, his design provided for wings to the east and to the west, which faced inwards onto rectangular courts. The final design for the new building took up the entire site of the old palace, its gardens

Portrait of George III, by Mather Brown (1761–1831), Private Collection / Photo © Christie's Images / The Bridgeman Art Library

and river front. The building was constructed beyond the line of the old Tudor wall out into the Thames.

There were many problems. Firstly, the ground sloped down from the Strand to the river almost 40 feet (12 metres). In Tudor times, the palace had gardens with steps leading down to the river. Sensibly, Chambers used

the drop for vaults providing storage space with a large terrace above. Watergates led under and into the building; the principal one is still visible today as the Great Arch. There were still houses on either side of the Strand entrance in private hands, therefore the frontage and entrance on that north side were very narrow compared with the rest of the building.

PROGRESS

Progress was slow and Chambers never saw his commission complete, dying in 1776. At his death, the estimate of £250,000 had risen to £500,000 and the foundations had just been laid for the Strand block; the scaffolding was removed from that frontage in 1779. By the end of that year much of the Strand block

was ready for occupancy by the learned societies. In fact, the first stage, designed by Chambers, was not finished until 1801, and even then a quarter of his original design had not been completed.

INSPIRATIONS

Chambers was an architect of his time, which meant that he was very alive to historical influence and his work on Somerset House demonstrates this. In common with many of his contemporaries he used the order of columns from ancient Greece, details of the Farnese Palace in Rome and, nearer home, certain motifs derived from Inigo Jones' work and details from old Somerset House itself in its original form as the first building in England in the English Renaissance style.

Keystone representing a River God

above: Sir Robert Smirke, by William Daniell; after George Dance (30 July 1809) © National Portrait Gallery, London

left: Courtyard of Somerset House, looking west, *circa* 1971–1996 © Angelo Hornak / CORBIS

a bust for the Society of Antiquaries, the second, a full-length bronze, can still be seen today in the courtyard.

Chambers' buildings were, above all, intended as offices and accommodation for the business of state and its civil servants, so he kept most of the interiors plain but he could not resist the temptation to run riot where the staircases were concerned. The staircase in the Royal Academy wing (now the Courtauld Gallery) wound steeply up the building with landings for 'stations of repose'. When Queen Charlotte visited the Exhibition Room, a chair was provided for her on each of these landings.

The Navy Staircase, now called the Nelson Stair, led to the Navy Office Boardroom, soaring magnificently into space over a sheer drop. This suffered bomb damage in 1940 but was carefully restored by Sir Albert Richardson. The Stamp Staircase, so called because it led to the stamp office is another example of Chambers' achievements in making the most out of what might have turned out to be a very dull set of government offices.

ENRICHMENTS

Chambers was friendly with many artists and sculptors and enlisted them to decorate the new building. On the courtyard side of the Strand block the statues 'of the attic' represent the four parts of the Globe and were executed by Mr Wilton. These were in celebration of Naval power and reflected the growing imperial ambitions of Britain at the time. Other carvings and reliefs, many with a marine motif, decorate the exterior of the building.

There were also two sculptures of George III by John Bacon. The first was

KING'S COLLEGE AND ROBERT SMIRKE

From 1801 Chambers' great design remained incomplete on the eastern and western sides of the great courtyard, and the east and west parts of the river front to the south. In 1826, however, the founders of King's College, amongst whom was the Duke of Wellington, applied to the government for a grant of the vacant land to the east of Somerset House and the site was made available on the condition that the College should be erected 'on a plan which would complete the river front of Somerset House at its eastern extremity in accordance with the original design of Sir William Chambers'. Sir Robert Smirke, architect of the British Museum and the Mint, was chosen and began work on the

The Opening
of the Victoria
Embankment, 1870
Museum of London

MR. JAMES PENNETHORNE.
Architect of the New Buildings for the London University, Burlington Gardens.

eastern side in 1829. In 1831, in spite of problems clearing the site, which had been used as a dumping ground by the government departments already in residence in the central site, the College was formally opened.

THE NEW WING AND JAMES PENNETHORNE

To complete Chambers' great work, and to provide room for the expansion of the Inland Revenue, James Pennethorne was asked to design a new wing which would complete the undeveloped part of the site, exposed to public view by the new Waterloo Bridge, built in 1817. The great strength of Pennethorne's design is that at its south end the New Wing ends twenty feet behind the river façade, thus the original proportions and intent of Chambers' monumental design were left undisturbed.

THE VICTORIA EMBANKMENT

Somerset House was first built by the Duke of Somerset partly because it gave him control of a riverside site from which he could journey to the city or Whitehall. In the 500 years of the existence of Somerset House, access to the river remained important. However, in 1864, the river finally ceded its dominance as a transport route to a series of Embankments. The Victoria Embankment, designed by Sir Joseph Bazalgette, destroyed Chambers' waterfront design at Somerset House. The Aberdeen granite base of his building was buried and the two smaller watergates became entrances from the new Embankment Road. The Great Arch – through which the Navy Commisioneri barge used to emerge – and the two barge houses were used for storage.

top: Sir James Pennethorne, *circa* 1870, after unknown artist
© National Portrait Gallery, London
above: Sir Joseph William Bazalgette, by Lock & Whitfield,
published 1877 © National Portrait Gallery, London

The Serlion Gates; part of Sir William Chambers' design, influenced by Inigo Jones © Country Life Picture Library / IPC Media

IV
THE PALACE OF ARTS AND LEARNING

When the crown finally relinquished old Somerset House to the government in 1774, George III, that most cultivated of kings, reserved the right to appropriate space in the new building for the Royal Academy of Arts, the Royal Society and the Society of Antiquaries.

George III, with the help of his childhood tutor and subsequent Prime Minister, Lord Bute, was a consummate collector of art. The purchases the two made in the earlier years of his reign, notably the 700-picture collection amassed by Joseph Smith, the British Consul in Venice, form a major part of the present Royal Collection. But George III was also a patron of art contemporary to his own time, and in 1768 Joshua Reynolds and William Chambers, backed by the King, formed the Royal Academy of Arts. The King did not like Reynolds, partly because he disagreed with his politics, but Reynolds was elected President, despite the King's preference for Chambers. When it came to obtaining permission in 1771 for the nascent Academy to use seven of the former state apartments in the crumbling old Somerset House, Chambers applied to his friend, the King, and it was done.

THE ROYAL ACADEMY SCHOOLS

Reynolds and his fellow artists founded the Royal Academy Schools to provide suitable teaching for a new generation. Students studied in the Plaster Academy and in the Life Class and they attended lectures every Monday night. J.M.W. Turner was one of the most famous students, elected an Associate of the Royal Academy in 1799 and a Royal Academician in 1802 at the age of 27.

THE GREAT EXHIBITION ROOM

At the top of Chambers' steep, winding staircase was the great exhibition room. Dr Johnson, a friend and supporter of Reynolds, went to the first pre-exhibition banquet there in 1780. 'The Exhibition! The Exhibition is eminently splendid. There is,' Dr Johnson told Mrs Thrale in his letter 'contour and keeping and grace and expression, and all the varieties of artificial excellence.' So popular was this annual exhibition that by 1821 there were 1,165 pictures in the show and these had to be hung from floor to ceiling. The last Royal Academy exhibition at Somerset House was held in 1836, when the Academy moved, first to what is now the National Gallery and eventually to Burlington House where it remains today. The most valuable of Chambers' decorations were taken down and re-used in both locations. The old rooms at Somerset House were taken over by the Department of Practical Art or Government School of Design.

top: Joshua Reynolds self portrait, *circa* 1779–80 © The Royal Academy of Arts, London
right: The Life School of the Royal Academy, Somerset House © The Royal Academy of Arts, London

top: Exhibition Room at Somerset House, 1808, by Thomas Rowlandson © The Royal Academy of Arts, London
above: Dr Syntax at the Exhibition, by Thomas Rowlandson © Private Collection

THE ROYAL SOCIETY

It was not only art that had a place in Chambers' revived and reinvented Somerset House; so, appropriately in the Age of Enlightenment, did science. The Royal Society is the oldest society in Britain, boasting such members as John Evelyn and Isaac Newton. In 1776, the Royal Society learnt that accommodation would be given to them by Chambers in his new Somerset House. The plan was for the three societies to occupy the two buildings on either side of the entrance from the Strand. The rest of his building, ranging along the north side of the courtyard was planned to house the Lottery Office, the Exchequer Office, Hawkers' and Pedlars' Offices and the Legacy Duty Office. This severely restricted the space for the Society, added to which it had been planned that The Royal Society and the Society of Antiquaries were to share the building to the east of the Strand entrance with a shared entrance and staircase, but separate apartments. There was a lot of to-ing and fro-ing about space, but The Royal Society gave way and held its Anniversary Meeting in its new premises in 1780.

A NEW PLANET

Auspiciously, one of the first discoveries on the part of a Fellow of The Royal Society in its new premises in Somerset House was the identification of a new planet in 1781 by William Herschel, the self-taught astronomer and professional musician. Wishing, in a politic manner, to name the new planet *Georgium Sidus* as a graceful acknowledgement to the King, wiser councils prevailed and it is now known as Uranus.

top left: Royal Academy Stare-case, *circa* 1808, by Thomas Rowlandson
above: 7 foot reflector Telescope which discovered Uranus, drawn by Sir William Watson © Royal Astronomical Society / Science Photo Lab
top right: Sir Isaac Newton, 1717, by Charles Jervas © The Royal Society

SCIENTIFIC DIPLOMACY

In the turbulent political days of the late 18th and early 19th century, members of the Royal Society acted as international mediators, preventing, through delicate diplomacy, war and politics from interfering with scientific discoveries. During the war with the American Colonies, for instance, Benjamin Franklin, a Fellow of The Royal Society since 1756, influenced the nascent American nation so that their warships should not interfere with Captain Cook on his last voyage of discovery. Later, during the Napoleonic Wars, which stretched from 1796–1815, that greatest of all naturalists, the genial President of

The Royal Society, Sir Joseph Banks, used his considerable influence in England and France to make sure that explorers of the two nations were not hindered by armies at war, and French scientists, rather incredibly, continued to be elected Fellows of the Society.

By 1820, when Sir Humphry Davy became President, the wars were over and the Society became re-oriented toward the pure scientific enquiry that was such a feature of the dawning age of the 19th century. The Royal Society remained at Somerset House until 1857 when it too decamped to Burlington House. Now it has handsome premises in Carlton House Terrace.

above: Portrait of Sir William Herschel, Astronomer Royal, after Lemuel Francis Abbott © Victoria Art Gallery, Bath and North East Somerset Council / The Bridgeman Art Library
left: Sir Joseph Banks, 1771–72, by Sir Joshua Reynolds © Agnew's, London, UK / The Bridgeman Art Library

Meeting of The Society of Antiquaries, 1812, by George Cruikshank © Society of Antiquaries of London

THE SOCIETY OF ANTIQUARIES

Founded in 1707 by Humphrey Wanley, then secretary to The Royal Society under Newton's presidency, The Society of Antiquaries is the oldest society of its kind in the world. It was founded at a time when, for the first time in history, the English began to have a sense of country and wanted to learn more of the past. Hearing in 1776 of the plans for the proposed new building, The Society of Antiquaries decided to enlist the support of King George III, their patron, in a bid for space in the new building. After some considerable politicking, which involved Chambers being asked to stand for election to the Society, the King was 'most graciously pleased' to order that the Society be accommodated with apartments in the new Buildings at Somerset House. When The Royal

Society moved out in 1857, the Antiquaries decided to remain. They, too, removed to Burlington House in 1874.

View of the Interior of Somerset House, Showing a Meeting of the Royal Antiquarian Society, *circa* 1840, by Frederick William Fairholt © Guildhall Library, City of London / The Bridgeman Art Library

V
THE COURTAULD INSTITUTE OF ART AND GALLERY

The Courtauld Institute of Art was founded in 1932 by Samuel Courtauld, a passionate art collector. His co-founders were Lord Lee of Fareham, the statesman and collector, and Sir Robert Witt the art historian.

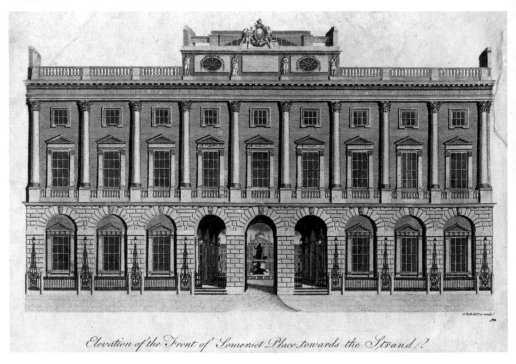

Elevation of the Front of Somerset Place, towards the Strand?

Entombment Triptych, *circa* 1410–1420, Master of Flemalle (Robert Campin?). © The Samuel Courtauld Trust, The Courtauld Gallery, London

SAMUEL COURTAULD'S COLLECTION

The core of the present collection was presented by Samuel Courtauld to the gallery in 1932. It consisted of French Impressionist and Post-Impressionist paintings and drawings. He made further gifts in the 1930s and a bequest in 1948. Samuel Courtauld's collection included Manet's *A Bar at the Folies Bergère* and a version of *Dejeuner sur l'Herbe*. Renoir is represented by *La Loge,* there are landscapes by Claude Monet and Camille Pissarro, a ballet scene by Edgar Degas and an incomparable group of eight major works by Cézanne. Samuel Courtauld also gave Van Gogh's *Self-Portrait with Bandaged Ear,* Gauguin's *Nevermore* and *Te Rerioa* and other important works by Seurat, Rousseau, Toulouse-Lautrec and Modigliani.

Samuel Courtauld's brother, Sir Stephen, was another collector. Known for his restoration of Eltham Palace where Henry VIII spent his childhood, he created a splendid Art Deco palace in the shell of the older building. In 1974, a group of thirteen Turner watercolours was presented to the gallery in his memory.

The Trinity with St Mary Magdalene and St John the Baptist, the Archangel Raphael and Tobias, 1490–1495, by Botticelli. © The Samuel Courtauld Trust, The Courtauld Gallery, London

27

OTHER SUPERLATIVE COLLECTIONS

The artist, art critic and collector Roger Fry was virtually single-handedly responsible for naming and bringing Post-Impressionist art to the attention of collectors in Britain in the 1910s. In 1934, the institute received his collection of 20th-century art. After the Second World War other collections were added, notably the collection of Old Master Paintings assembled by Lord Lee, including Cranach's *Adam and Eve*. Sir Robert Witt, the third in the triumvirate of founders, bequeathed his important collection of Old Master and British drawings in 1952. Mark Gambier-Parry contributed the collection of art formed by his grandfather. This represented an earlier era of connoisseur collecting at its apogee with the *kunstkammer* collections of the princely families of 15th–18th-century Europe, ranging as it did from early Italian Renaissance painting to majolica, medieval enamels, ivory carvings and other art forms.

THE COLLECTION OF COUNT ANTOINE SEILERN

Other great collectors have followed suit in contributing to the incomparable richness of the Courtaulds holdings. In 1978, it received the Princes Gate Collection of Old Master paintings and drawings formed by Count Antoine Seilern. This is generally acknowledged to be one of the greatest collections formed in Britain in the 20th century. Count Antoine Seilern was intensely private, and his rarely-visited collection was housed at his home in Princes Gate.

The part of the collection now in the possession of the Courtauld includes works by Breugel, Quentin Matsys, Van Dyck and Tiepolo, and is strongest in the works of Rubens. The collection also included works by Pissarro, Degas, Renoir and Oskar Kokoschka.

above: Triptych: The Descent from the Cross (centre panel), 1611, Peter Paul Rubens © The Samuel Courtauld Trust, The Courtauld Gallery, London

left: Adam and Eve, 1526, by Lucas Cranach the Elder © The Samuel Courtauld Trust, The Courtauld Gallery, London

Bar at the Folies-Bergère, 1882, by Edouard Manet © The Samuel Courtauld Trust, The Courtauld Gallery, London

THE COURTAULD INSTITUTE OF ART

The Courtauld is a self-governing college of the University of London specialising in the study of the history of art, conservation and curating, with a world-class reputation and international reach. It has many distinguished alumni, including the directors of the British Museum, the National Gallery, Victoria & Albert Museum, Tate and New York's Metropolitan Museum of Art, the novelist and art historian Anita Brookner, the Turner Prize winning artist Jeremy Deller, and the Canadian artist-photographer Jeff Wall.

LEARNING

The Courtauld's distinguished faculty teaches over 400 BA, MA and research students. Its excellent resources include one of the largest archives of art historical books, periodicals and exhibition catalogues in the UK. It houses two photographic libraries which started as private collections (the Conway library covers architecture, architectural drawings, sculpture and illuminated manuscripts, and the Witt library of paintings, drawings and engravings) and the Samuel Courtauld Trust's collection of paintings, drawings, prints, sculpture and decorative arts, much of which is displayed in The Courtauld Gallery and is accessible via an online image collection. The Courtauld also offers a range of public programmes and short courses.

Having insisted that part of the new Somerset House should become a centre of art and learning, George III would approve of this 21st-century version of the Age of Enlightenment.

Self-portrait with bandaged ear, 1889, Vincent van Gogh © The Samuel Courtauld Trust, The Courtauld Gallery, London

VI
THE PALACE OF EMPIRE

In inheriting old Somerset House, the government of the day made the decision to turn the ruined royal palace into an entirely new building in this very central location for important government offices.

Navy Office Somerset House, London. Published 1825 by J. Taylor, High Holborn

THE CIVIL SERVICE AT SOMERSET HOUSE

Hitherto, civil service offices had been scattered about the palace of Whitehall and its surroundings. This centralisation continued from the time Sir William Chambers was commissioned to design this new civil service administrative headquarters up to the present day, with the offices of The Board of the Inland Revenue still occupying the west wing and part of the new wing.

In 1785, the Audit Office began its tenancy in the east wing, which also provided space for various other offices. Four years later, the Stamp Office, the Navy Office, the Navy Pay Office, the Victualling Office and the Sick and Wounded Office had been housed in the south and west wings and other offices in the wings of the north wing. In 1834, the Poor Law Commission and the office of the Tithe and Copyhold Commissioners also came to Somerset House, being accommodated in the north wing.

THE NAVY BOARD

For nearly a century, over a third of Somerset House was occupied by the various branches of the Navy Board, who were conspicuously successful in reorganising and administering the Navy. By 1805 and the Battle of Trafalgar, Britain had beaten the fleets of France, Spain, Holland and Denmark and had blockaded the coast of Europe.

Since the time of Henry VIII, who founded it in 1546, a year after he lost his flagship the *Mary Rose*, the Navy Board had been responsible for the civil administration of the Naval under the Lord High Admiral. At the Restoration in 1660, the Navy Board was reconstituted under four principal officers and three commissioners. From 1660 to 1688, the office of Clerk of the Acts (previously Clerk of the Ships) was held by the diarist Samuel

Pepys. During the 1670s, Pepys and his fellow officers' efficiency laid the groundwork of British naval supremacy for the next century.

But at the beginning of the 18th century the Navy Board was inconveniently over two miles distant from the Admiralty, being situated in Seething Lane behind the Tower of London, thus to move it virtually next door to the Admiralty was a sensible decision.

Chambers housed the Navy Board on the west side of the south wing facing the river. Related offices occupied the buildings on the west side of the courtyard and the central Seamen's Waiting Hall doubled up as a very grand entrance to the Navy Board and its various appendages. Here, captains on half-pay might have been found, hoping to be given a new ship. Suppliers of food and equipment to the Navy would also have passed through

the Seamens' Hall, as would Maurice Nelson, the Admiral's brother who worked there for most of his life, ending as Chief Clerk.

The great apartment in the centre of the south wing was devoted to a permanent exhibition of models of typical ships and other objects, illustrating the history, progress and importance of the Navy. It was a very popular attraction, open daily and, until the collection was removed to Greenwich, brought the public into Somerset House for the first time in two centuries. On Sundays, the terrace overlooking the Thames, possibly the finest promenade in London, was also open to the public. Visitors included the editor Herbert Spencer, who borrowed a key to the terrace and walked there often with Mary Anne Lewis – who wrote under the name George Eliot.

Lord Nelson, by Sir William Beechey (1753–1839) © Cider House Galleries, Ltd., Bletchingley, Surrey, UK / The Bridgeman Art Library

ADMIRAL LORD NELSON

The Navy Board was extremely important, if not vital, to those wishing to become officers in the Navy. Hundreds of midshipmen came to Somerset House annually to try to pass for the rank of lieutenant before the Board. Among these midshipmen was Horatio Nelson who, at the age of twelve, passed through London on his way to his first ship at Chatham. Later, as a young officer, he lived in Salisbury Street, south of the Strand. Much later, a member of the Audit office remembered, 'I was in the habit of seeing for many mornings a thin, spare naval officer with only one arm enter the vestibule at a smart step and make direct for the Admiralty over the rough paving stones of the Quadrangle instead of taking… the smooth paving at the sides. His thin,

Unloading *The Illustrated London News* at the Somerset House Stamp Office

frail figure shook at every step and I often wondered why he chose so rough a footway but I ceased to wonder when I heard that the thin, frail officer was no other than Lord Nelson'.

In 1832, the Napoleonic Wars being over, the Navy and Victualling Boards were both abolished and their functions transferred to the Navy under the supervision of the Admiralty Board.

The Nelson Stair at Somerset House © James Brittain

The Model Ship Museum, 1842, by T.H. Shepherd

New Registry of Wills Office
at Somerset House, *circa* 1875
© Westminster City Archives

THE INLAND REVENUE

One of the most lucrative ways the government in the 18th century raised revenue was by charging stamp duty on documents. This was administered by the Stamp Office which, in 1789, moved to the new Somerset House. In the days when stamp duty was imposed on newspapers the Quadrangle was a maelstrom of stamping; every news-sheet issued throughout the kingdom had to be stamped by hand, so carts rumbled daily through the Strand gate bringing in bales of paper intended for the press.

In 1834, the Stamp Office amalgamated with the Affairs of Taxes, and in 1849 both joined the Excise to form a new Board of Inland Revenue which still occupies part of the east wing and some of the west wing of Somerset House.

THE GENERAL REGISTER OFFICE

Up until the time of the creation of the General Register Office, records of births, marriages and deaths were recorded in parish or church registers, the latter having been ordered to be kept by Henry VIII, but such registers were very unreliable. In 1836, the General Register Office was formed under the rule of the Registrar General and was based at Somerset House, where it remained until 1970, when it moved out. It now operates in various locations under the Home Office.

THE PRINCIPAL PROBATE REGISTRY

All wills, whether originals or copies, had to be registered at the Principal Probate Registry from 1857. In 1874, the Registry moved to Somerset House. It moved out in 1973. It has in its files extraordinary wills including

that of Shakespeare, who left his wife 'my second best bed with the furniture'. Here may also be found Jane Austen's will, William Penn's will and, until it was returned to France, the will of Napoleon.

Jane Austen, *circa* 1810,
by Cassandra Austen
© National Portrait Gallery, London

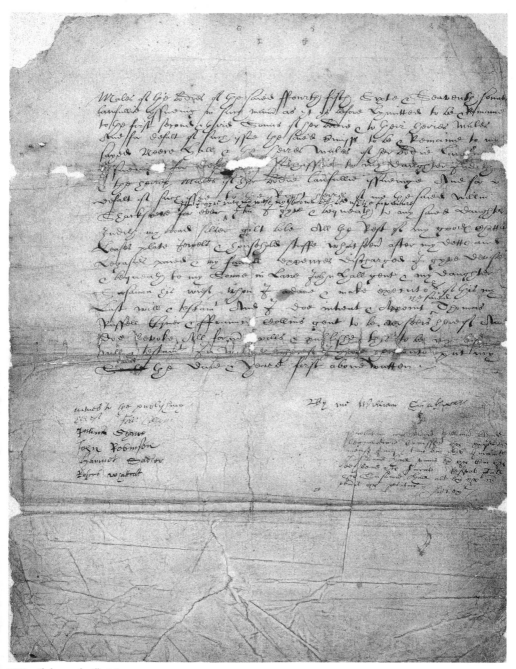

William Shakespeare's will, 1616
The National Archives, Kew

VII
THE 21ST-CENTURY PALACE

For the better part of 150 years, Somerset House was the secret beehive of Empire – the province of various branches of the Civil Service. It became a very private palace, virtually unknown to the public.

The Somerset House courtyard during building work © Lucinda Rogers

THE PRESENT DAY

Somerset House suffered bomb damage in 1940 and in 1941. The south wing took several hits and the Nelson staircase and Naval Boardroom were damaged. Modernisation and repair work after the war destroyed parts of the original joinery and decoration and the handsomely proportioned rooms were often sub-divided by mezzanines. The courtyard was covered in tarmac and used as a car park for civil servants working in the building.

THE SLEEPING PALACE CAMPAIGN

In 1977, Simon Jenkins, then Editor of the *Evening Standard*, started a campaign in his newspaper to 'wake up the sleeping palace on the Thames' telling his readers that Somerset House could be theirs to enjoy and that the Civil Service should move, leaving the Strand and river wings to be used for art galleries, for chamber concerts and other uses. Jenkins also suggested that on summer evenings, the courtyard might be used for *Son et Lumiere*.

It took nearly 30 years and a succession of ministers who inherited the project then let it lapse, before Somerset House once again saw the public not just being allowed to walk through the courtyard and along the river terrace but positively encouraged to become familiar with its extraordinary architecture, its beauty, and the peace which the poet Thomas Crabbe found in its environs.

The Registrar of Births Marriages and Deaths moved out of the north wing in 1973, leaving it vacant. The Courtauld Institute of Art moved into the restored buildings in 1990.

SOMERSET HOUSE TRUST

IN 1997, the Somerset House Trust was formed in order to maintain the Somerset House buildings for the public and to provide a centre for arts and culture. These aims were financed by the rent obtained mainly from the Inland Revenue who remained in the new, west and east wings negotiated by Michael Heseltine, the Minister responsible at the time. At that juncture, Somerset House was envisaged as being partly a permanent museum quarter, the core of which would be the Courtauld Gallery.

In 2000 Somerset House was re-opened to the public with the north and south wings open and

the courtyard restored to its former elegance with the installation of the first public fountain commission for 60 years. The Edmond J.Safra Fountain Court has the centrepiece of 55 illuminated and choreographed fountains set into granite setts.

THE GILBERT COLLECTION AND THE HERMITAGE ROOMS

Lord Rothschild, then Chairman of the Heritage Lottery Fund, negotiated with Sir Arthur Gilbert a gift to the nation of his collection of gold, silver and micro-mosaic objects. The vaulted spaces of the Embankment building adjacent to the south wing were converted into a gallery to display the collection, supported by the Heritage Lottery Fund. Subsequently, it was decided to move the Gilbert Collection to the Victoria & Albert Museum, a more appropriate museum for its study and appreciation.

To further the aim of establishing Somerset House as a museum quarter, five galleries in the south wing were specially decorated to recreate the atmosphere and the

The Edmond J. Safra Fountain Court at Somerset House

aesthetics of the Hermitage Museum in St. Petersburg and were devoted to loan exhibitions from the museum. Now, of the original five rooms, two remain as offices, not open to the public, to further the aims of the Hermitage. The other three rooms have become a suite for free small public displays.

A CULTURAL BEEHIVE

If being one of the centres of the administration of a global Empire was the role of Somerset House in the 19th and 20th centuries, in the 21st century this grand building which looks like a palace but cleverly conceals the fact that it was built as offices, is assuming a new role in beginning to create a cultural community. Offices are used by a combination of both established and pioneering new talent within the cultural sector. In addition the vaults around the courtyard are being colonised as studio spaces for artists and designers to stimulate creativity on the site. Somerset House, once the centre of creative and scholarly endeavour through the Royal Academy and Royal Society, is once again playing a role in the life of cultural London in the new millenium.

THE SORRELL FOUNDATION YOUNG DESIGN CENTRE

The Sorrell Foundation Young Design Centre opened in Somerset House in spring 2007. The aim of the Centre is to explore what young people want from design at school and in their daily lives. It presents exhibitions and events, runs creative workshops and supports young people's contribution to the conversation about design in their environment. *What's Next For Schools* is an innovative interactive display that describes what pupils want in their schools.

THE ROYAL SOCIETY OF LITERATURE

The Royal Society of Literature is one of the cultural tenants of Somerset House. It was founded in 1820 by George IV to 'reward literary merit and excite literary talent'. Past Fellows of the society include Coleridge, Keats, Kipling and Thomas Hardy; present fellows include V.S. Naipaul, Martin Amis and Tom Stoppard. The Royal Society of Literature offers a varied programme of free lectures for members and their guests and to the public.

Film4 Summer Screen at Somerset House
© David Parry

SOMERSET HOUSE ACTIVE

In the past five years, there has been a radical change of direction in terms of what Somerset House offers the public. No longer conceived of as being a static museum quarter, it is now playing an increasing role as a centre of culture in the capital, through, among other initiatives, a challenging programme of temporary exhibitions focusing on contemporary fashion, architecture, art and design planned to provide a unique platform for contemporary manifestations of creativity and thought. These take place in the Embankment Galleries, which formerly housed the Gilbert Collection.

Somerset House Ice Rink © Crispin Hughes

Skin+Bones at Somerset House
© Richard Bryant

LONDON FASHION WEEK

There is a varied programme of activities throughout the year. The Summer Series offers a season of summertime outdoor concerts, held in the Edmond J. Safra Fountain Court. Film4 Summer Screen attracts audiences to open-air film screenings throughout August. In the winter, the courtyard becomes the grandest skating rink in the world for Skate at Somerset House.

London Fashion Week will find its new home in Somerset House in autumn 2009, providing an extraordinary backdrop for cutting edge contemporary British fashion creativity and a nucleus for other smaller scale fashion exhibitions in the future.

WHAT TO DO AND SEE AT SOMERSET HOUSE

1 THE COURTAULD INSTITUTE OF ART
One of the world's leading centres for the study of art history and conservation. The collection and the Witt Library are exceptional resources for the Institute's students, many of whom go on to fill prestigious international positions as curators, scholars, critics, artists and dealers.

2 THE COURTAULD GALLERY
An internationally renowned small museum of art. Its collection stretches from the early Renaissance into the 20th century and is particularly renowned for its unrivalled collection of Impressionist and Post-Impressionist paintings. The Gallery also holds an outstanding collection of drawings and prints and fine examples of sculpture and decorative arts.

3 THE STATUE OF GEORGE III
A stylised image of George III as a Roman helmsman, with Father Thames reclining below. It was designed to reinforce and emphasise the maritime power of Georgian Britain.

4 THE EDMOND J. SAFRA FOUNTAIN COURT
One of the most architecturally stunning courtyards in central London. The water jets rising from the granite paving perform special displays on the hour and half hour during the summer months between 10am–11pm. At night the courtyard and fountains are transformed with beautiful architectural lighting.

5 THE LIGHTWELLS AND DEADHOUSE
Explore the airy lightwells, atmospheric Deadhouse and other architectural treasures with our free guided tours. You'll find evidence of Tudor intrigue and Georgian Enlightenment, scientific curiosity and naval power.

6 THE SEAMEN'S HALL
The heart of the old Navy Board is now the main entrance to Somerset House. The majestic, neo-classical hall now houses a contemporary visitor information and reception desk, and lounge area.

7 THE NELSON STAIR
William Chambers' dramatically soaring staircase, which imitates a stair on a ship. Originally called the Navy Stair, and designed as the approach to Navy Office Boardroom, it was later renamed after Lord Nelson and suffered severely from bomb damage during World War II.

8 THE STAMP STAIR
An elegant stair built to access the Stamp Office – the beginnings of the Inland Revenue. It is interesting to note that as the staircase descends towards the basement, where the printing machines were housed, the architectural detailing becomes plainer and more rustic in style, signifying the lower status of the labourers working there.

9 THE TERRACE ROOMS
These three elegant rooms, originally part of the Stamp Office, overlook the River Terrace and house free, changing public displays.

10 THE RESTAURANT, CAFÉ AND BAR
Situated in rooms that used to house the Navy offices, these bright, elegant spaces have views onto the River Terrace. The restaurant menu is designed for relaxed dining featuring simple dishes using seasonal produce. The delicatessen offers a range of fair trade and organic take-away food and drink.

11 THE RIVER TERRACE AND CAFÉ
Dine al fresco in the stylish café/bar and enjoy the magnificent views captured by Canaletto. The majestic 18th-century façade of Somerset House towers above. Below is the sweep of the Thames from St Paul's Cathedral to the London Eye and Houses of Parliament, offering one of the most beautiful vantage points of the river in London.

12 EMBANKMENT GALLERIES
The vaulted spaces to the east and west of the Great Arch, that were once used as stores and barge houses, are now home to temporary exhibitions galleries focussing on contemporary fashion, architecture, art and design.

13 GREAT ARCH
Somerset House was effectively isolated from Whitehall and the Admiralty Office by the slums that stretched from Charing Cross to the Savoy, so the easiest route was by barge. Somerset House had its own front door on the River – the Great Arch, through which barges would load; the Navy Board's own ornate gilded barge would sail up river to Whitehall or down river to the dockyards at Deptford or Woolwich.

14 OLD PALACE EXHIBITION
Situated in the gallery below the Great Arch, a multimedia presentation and display explains the evolution of Somerset House, from its origins as a Tudor Palace. Also on display is one of the few surviving examples of the Navy Commissioners' barges used by the Lords Commissioners of the Admiralty travelling up and down river.

15 THE LEARNING CENTRE
Housed in vaulted spaces formerly used as laundries and wash houses, the Learning Centre is a series of purpose-built studio rooms and presentation spaces that host a range of year-round workshops and activities for families, young people and adults, with an emphasis on the visual arts and design. The centre is a lively hub for formal and informal learning during term-time and the holidays.

Right: Somerset House
© Country Life Picture Library / IPC Media
Overleaf: Somerset House Map